It is not good to be careless.

It is better for you to be careful.

Be careful.

DO NOT PLAY IN DANGEROUS PLACES.

If you avoid playing in dangerous places,
you will avoid hurting yourself and others.

Be careful.

DO NOT PLAY WITH DANGEROUS THINGS.

If you avoid playing with dangerous things,
you will avoid hurting yourself and others.

Be careful.

DO NOT PLAY TOO ROUGHLY.

Someone might get hurt, or something might get broken if you play too roughly.

No one will get hurt, and nothing will get broken if you play carefully.

Be careful.

LISTEN TO THE PEOPLE AND SOUNDS
AROUND YOU.

They may be warning you that danger is near.
If you listen and respond to them, you may
avoid a dangerous situation.

Be careful.

LOOK WHERE YOU ARE GOING.

If you do, you will avoid tripping and bumping into things.

Be careful.

SLOW DOWN.

If you do, you will avoid the accidents that often happen when you are in a hurry.

Be careful.

PAY ATTENTION.

Think about what you are doing. If you do, you will make fewer mistakes.

Be careful.

OBEY THE RULES.

The adults who are responsible for you know what you need to do to keep yourself and others safe. They also know what you need to do to take care of the things around you.

The rules they make can help you to be careful.

It is not good to be careless.

You need to BE CAREFUL instead.

When you are careful you act as though you care about yourself.

When you are careful you act as though you care about the people and things around you.

Being careless can cause you to damage
or destroy something.

Being careless can cause you to hurt other people.

Being careless can cause you to hurt yourself.

You are being careless when you act as though you do not care about yourself.

You are being careless when you act as though you do not care about the people and things around you.

Let's talk about BEING CARELESS.

Let's Talk About
BEING CARELESS

Illustrated by John Costanza
Edited by Kate Dickey
Designed by Abigail Johnston

GROLIER ENTERPRISES CORP.

Grolier Enterprises Inc. offers a varied selection of both adult and children's book racks. For details on ordering, please write: Grolier Enterprises Inc., Sherman Turnpike, Danbury, CT 06816, Attn: Premium Department.

Let's Talk About
BEING CARELESS